Steck-Va

WORLD MYTHS

The Labors of Heracles

Reviewer
Daniel H. Garrison
Associate Professor of Classics
Northwestern University

STECK-VAUGHN
C O M P A N Y
A Subsidiary of National Education Corporation

Europe

Black Sea

<u>Ancient Greece</u>

Asia

Crete
Sea

Mediterranean Sea

Africa

Introduction

The ancient Greeks were a curious and adventurous people. They were not always content to stay in their small, mountainous land. The Greek city-states established colonies and spread Greek culture all over the shores of the Mediterranean Sea.

As you might expect, the many heroes of Greek myths traveled, too. This is true of the hero Heracles (HAYR uh kleez), whom the Romans later called Hercules (HER kyoo leez). Many of the adventures that people call "the labors of Heracles" happened in Greece itself. Others took Heracles to the frontiers of the Greek world.

The Greeks drew a clear line between human beings, who were mortal, and the gods, who were immortal. The heroes were considered mortal, although most of them had one parent who was a god. Only the hero Heracles, was great enough to join the most powerful gods who lived on Mount Olympus despite the fact that his mother was a mortal.

Ancient stories and paintings show many different sides of Heracles. Sometimes he seems as mean and violent as the monsters he conquers. At others times, he appears to be the perfect example of what a human should be. Sometimes he is completely free, and sometimes he must serve others. Most often, the Greeks treat him as a serious hero. But he can also play funny roles. What different sides of Heracles do you see in the story of his labors that follows? From reading about Heracles, what traits do you think the Greeks admired in human beings?

THE LABORS
of HERACLES

Heracles (HAYR uh kleez) was the finest of all the Greek heroes. He was half human and half god. His father was Zeus (zoos), king of the gods. Being Zeus' son made Heracles both great and famous, but it didn't help him as much as you might think. You see, being a son of Zeus meant having the jealous queen, Hera (HAYR uh), for a stepmother. Hera hated Heracles from the moment he was born. She even sent a pair of serpents to attack him as he slept in his cradle. Fortunately, Heracles showed his powers at an early age and strangled the huge snakes in his chubby little fists.

After this spectacular beginning, Heracles grew up to be unbelievably strong. And he did many heroic deeds. But Hera always seemed to be lurking around, waiting to cause problems for him. Once, Hera drove Heracles crazy enough to commit murder. When the madness passed, Heracles was filled with remorse. That wasn't enough, though. Even Zeus agreed that Heracles should be punished. And so the mighty Heracles was made the servant of Eurystheus (yoo RISS thee uhs), who was king of Tiryns (TIR inz). As kings went, Eurystheus was a cowardly nobody, but he felt very important at the thought of having the great Heracles in his power. Heracles didn't like the idea of serving Eurystheus, but what could he do?

Anyway, prompted by the goddess Hera, King Eurystheus announced that he would give Heracles twelve tasks, or labors, mostly of the monster-slaying sort. Both Hera and Eurystheus hoped her stepson would at least be humiliated, and perhaps even destroyed, by these labors.

When Heracles heard about them, though, he began to relax. After all, how could a few monsters bother someone who had strangled two snakes in his cradle? Besides, Heracles was eager to win some glory and possibly help out the people of Greece. So, shaking his club and other heroic weapons, he marched right up to the throne in Eurystheus' palace. "All right, Eurystheus, let's get on with it. What is the first labor going to be?"

"I heard recently," said the king, "that a lion is causing trouble in the countryside near Nemea (NEM ee uh). It's eating livestock and even people. How about tackling that?"

"Just a lion?" responded Heracles, a bit disappointed. "Don't you have something a little more challenging?"

"Oh, this is hardly 'just a lion,'" said Eurystheus, chuckling. "I have no doubt that you'll find it quite a challenge."

Shrugging his shoulders, Heracles strode off to Nemea to seek out the lion. When he crept up on the lion chewing bones in its den, he put an arrow to his bow and fired. His aim was true, all right, and the arrow hit the lion where it should have. But the trouble was that the arrow bounced right off the beast's hide! Heracles sat down to think. If arrows wouldn't work, neither would clubs or spears.

"I guess I'll have to wrestle it," thought our hero, who was clever as well as strong. With that, he leaped onto the back of the brute, wrapped his arms and legs around it, and squeezed. In no time at all, the fearsome lion had gone permanently limp, so Heracles threw it across his back and returned to Tiryns. Eurystheus was so terrified at the mere sight of the lion's body that he jumped into a bronze urn and refused to come out. "From now on, Heracles," he squeaked from his urn, "you are to leave your trophies outside the city gates!"

"We'll see," said Heracles with a chuckle, as he skinned the lion with its own razor-sharp claws. "What's next?"

The next task was the conquering of the Hydra (HIE druh) of Lerna (LER nuh). This Hydra was a truly awesome monster! Picture nine poison-spitting heads on nine snake-like necks, all attached to one body, and you'll have the idea. Wearing his new lion skin tied across his shoulders, Heracles marched right up to the Hydra and attacked. To his distress, he found that as soon as he cut off one head, two more grew in its place. To make matters worse, one head seemed to be immortal. Even Heracles had to admit that the Hydra might be too much for him to handle alone. He just didn't have enough arms and legs to fight all the heads at once. So he summoned a friend to help. "Every time I cut off a head," said the hero, "touch the wound with this burning torch. That will keep the heads from growing back."

The idea worked
like magic. When the mortal
heads were dead, Heracles buried the
immortal one under a rock where it couldn't
do any more damage.
    Of course, Eurystheus was stunned when Heracles returned
in one piece from his battle with the Hydra. But the king didn't
let Heracles see how surprised he was. Instead, he gave Heracles
his next two assignments.

Labor number three was to bring back alive an incredibly swift deer with golden horns. The deer was called the Cerynean (ser IN ee uhn) Hind. Heracles could have shot it easily, but catching it was nearly impossible. This deer was so fast that it led our hero on a merry chase for a whole year before he was able to trap it with nets!

No sooner had Heracles come panting back to Tiryns with his latest trophy than he was off on the fourth labor. This time he had to rid the Earth of yet another monstrous pest. A huge boar was running wild on the slopes of Mount Erymanthus (ayr uh MAN thuhs). Heracles cleverly drove it into the deep mountain snow. There it lay thrashing and snorting, until Heracles rescued it and carried it off alive to Tiryns. One look at it sent Eurystheus scurrying back to his urn, but that didn't stop him from coming up with the fifth labor.

Though this labor was not particularly dangerous, it was totally disgusting. It seemed that King Augeas (oj EE uhs), who ruled Elis (EE lis), was rich in cattle—to put it mildly. He had so many animals in his stables that it was impossible to clean up after them. The mess had become unbearable. King Eurystheus had volunteered Heracles' help for this nasty chore. "Why, Augeas, it should be no trouble at all for my servant Heracles to take care of your little problem!" volunteered Eurystheus, who thought this labor would be especially humiliating to the hero.

As usual, things did not turn out the way Eurystheus had planned. The son of Zeus was not about to do the job of cleaning out the Augean (oj EE uhn) Stables with a mere shovel. Once again, Heracles proved that he was the worthy offspring of his brilliant father. As he gazed at the awful stables and thought about his problem, he noticed two rivers flowing nearby. He

could use them to accomplish the deed! First he broke down one wall of the stables. Then he changed the course of the rivers so that they flowed right through the filthy mess. In less time than it takes to tell of this task, the foul stables were flushed clean—and Heracles had barely muddied his hands. On his way home, he stopped in the pleasant valley of Olympia and founded the Olympic games to honor his father Zeus.

"Well," crowed Heracles, standing once more before Eurystheus, "five labors down, seven to go! What do you have in store for me next? I'd like to do something more helpful to ordinary people than cleaning royal stables."

"All right," Eurystheus snapped. He was growing sick of seeing Heracles return triumphantly from labor after labor. "Over in Arcadia (ar CAY dee uh) there is a marsh where you will find so many noisy birds that the people there can't hear their own thoughts. Get rid of them!"

This Heracles did, once more using his mind as well as his body. When he reached the marsh, he was astounded to find it completely hidden beneath a huge blanket of squawking birds. With a brass rattle that he had made himself, he raised such a hideous racket that the birds took flight in terror and never returned.

Again Eurystheus was forced to watch the heroic son of Zeus strolling up to the palace with hardly a wrinkle in his lion-skin cloak. "He is back much too soon," fumed Eurystheus. "I must send him farther away!"

And so the next three labors took our hero beyond the Greek mainland. The seventh labor sent him to the island of Crete to pick up a bull that was destroying farms and villages. He delivered it, as ordered, to Tiryns.

The eighth labor was much grimmer. Diomedes (die uh MEE deez) ruled Thrace, north of Greece. Unlike the friendly Greeks, he did not welcome visitors with open arms. In fact, as soon as any strangers set foot in his kingdom, Diomedes fed them to his herd of bloodthirsty mares. Heracles captured the mares easily and turned the tables on this evil king. Heracles made that part of the world much safer for travelers.

Labor number nine was a bit different. King Eurystheus' spoiled daughter had a great desire to own the golden belt of Hippolyta (hip OL it uh), who was queen of the Amazons (AM uh zonz). The Amazons were a nation of warrior women who lived along the south shore of the Black Sea. When Eurystheus's daughter learned that Heracles had to do whatever her father ordered, she persuaded him to send the hero after the belt.

With a few friends, Heracles set off. Our hero got along well with the fierce women, although he had feared their violence. Hippolyta graciously agreed to give up the golden belt. Unfortunately, the goddess Hera was annoyed that her stepson had gotten the prize without a struggle, so she spread a rumor that Heracles had kidnapped Hippolyta. And so, a battle broke out, and Heracles was forced to grab the belt and run. This time, Eurystheus welcomed his return since it put a quick stop to his daughter's whining.

That left three labors for the son of Zeus to complete. What Eurystheus and Hera had in mind would have been overwhelming to anyone but Heracles. All three labors took him to the western edge of the world, to places covered in night and death.

For the tenth labor, the son of Zeus was sent to an island ruled by Geryon (JAY ree uhn), to bring back his herd of cattle. Geryon was a triple-threat monster—he had three bodies. On his way to the island, Heracles cut a channel through the narrow stretch of land where Africa met Spain, and thus joined the Atlantic Ocean and the Mediterranean Sea. Finally, arriving at Geryon's kingdom, he killed the monster in record time and came back to Tiryns in triumph.

The hero had hardly had time for a refreshing bath when Eurystheus explained labor eleven. In northwest Africa, in the garden of the nymphs called Hesperides (hes PAYR uh deez), grew a tree with golden apples. It was guarded by a fierce serpent. Heracles was to retrace his steps to that part of the world and steal the apples.

Once again the son of Zeus set off. But before he reached the garden, Heracles stopped to chat with his distant relative, the giant Atlas (AT luhs). Atlas' duty was to hold up the sky on his shoulders. Seeing a chance to escape his burden, Atlas offered to steal the golden apples if only Heracles would hold up the sky for a few minutes. Heracles agreed, and held up the sky while Atlas left. Atlas quickly returned with the apples. "These apples are pretty heavy," Atlas said slyly. "Why don't I just deliver them to Eurystheus myself and save you the trouble?"

Heracles saw right through this scheme. He had no intention of holding up the sky forever, so he played a trick of his own. "Sure," he replied innocently. "I'll tell you what, just hold

this for a second while I
get a pillow for my shoulders.
Then you can take off for Tiryns."

Foolish Atlas! Congratulating
himself on his cleverness, he took back the sky—
and watched in fury as Heracles snatched up the apples and
dashed away.

Once in Tiryns again, Heracles found that the king had
saved the worst labor for last. The twelfth one was the most
terrifying of all, for it meant a journey to the Underworld, ruled
by the frightful god Hades (HAY deez). Heracles' mission was to
fetch Cerberus (SER ber uhs), the triple-headed, snake-tailed
guard dog of the dead. Now Cerberus wasn't any more
dangerous than the Nemean Lion and the Hydra. The problem
was where the dog lived. The path to the Underworld was a one-
way street—going down was easy, but returning was impossible.
Still, if anybody could do it, Heracles could.

Again our hero traveled West. This time he went to the entrance of the lower world. When he had descended through crowds of ghosts to Hades' palace, he met with the grim god of the dead and made a deal. "Lord Hades," he said, "I am Heracles, son of your brother Zeus. As a favor to him, would you let me borrow your dog, Cerberus, for a little while? I promise to return him in good condition."

"Well," replied the god, not wanting to lend his watchdog, but unwilling to anger Zeus, "I guess you may, as long as you catch him without using any weapons." Hades was quite sure the hero would fail.

Naturally, Hades was wrong. Heracles had plenty of experience wrestling monsters, so it was easy for him to grab Cerberus and squeeze just hard enough to knock him out. For the last time, Heracles dragged a trophy back to Tiryns. As he

lifted the dog up to show Eurystheus, the brute woke up and began to growl and snap. The king turned green and dove into his urn again. "You can take Cerberus back now," whimpered Eurystheus. "I know him when I see him."

"Not so fast," shouted Heracles, holding the snarling dog up to the mouth of the urn. "Either you swear that I have finished my labors, or I turn Cerberus loose."

"All right, all right, I swear," stammered the king. "You have fulfilled your obligation. Now go."

And so Heracles completed his labors and paid for his crime. But that didn't end his work as a hero. For the rest of his life, he protected people by ridding the world of frightening beasts. And many believed that, in the end, his hard work earned him a reward most unusual for Greek heroes. They say that, after his death, Heracles was admitted to the company of the immortal gods on Mount Olympus.

Glossary

city-state *n.* An independent city and the surrounding area that it controls.   p. 3

commit *v.* To do or act; to perform.   p. 5

course *n.* The direction or path something or someone takes.   p. 9

nymph *n.* In Greek myths, one of many goddesses of nature.   p. 12

obligation *n.* A duty or promise to do something.   p. 15

offspring *n.* Child or children of someone.   p. 8

remorse *n.* Deep regret for having done something wrong.   p. 5

stepmother *n.* A woman married to one's father who is not one's mother.   p. 4

trait *n.* A quality or element of someone's character or personality.   p. 3

Underworld *n.* In Greek myths, the lower world or place thought to be the kingdom of the dead.   p. 13

urn *n.* A large vase or jar, often used for storage.   p. 6

Acknowledgments

Steck-Vaughn Company

Executive Editor Diane Sharpe
Senior Editor Martin S. Saiewitz
Assistant Art Director Cynthia Ellis

Proof Positive/Farrowlyne Associates, Inc.

Program Development, Design, and Production

Illustration

Roberta Collier-Morales